W9-CZL-900

Big

Science Ideas

What is a Vertebrate?

Bobbie Kalman

🌱 Crabtree Publishing Company

www.crabtreebooks.com

Big Science Ideas

Created by Bobbie Kalman

Dedicated by Katherine Kantor
To the Kovac family—with all my love.

Author and Editor-in-Chief
Bobbie Kalman

Editors
Reagan Miller
Robin Johnson

Photo research
Crystal Sikkens

Design
Bobbie Kalman
Katherine Kantor
Samantha Crabtree (cover)

Production coordinator
Katherine Kantor

Illustrations
Barbara Bedell: pages 1, 11, 13, 15 (mudpuppy), 23, 24, 25
Antoinette "Cookie" Bortolon: page 9 (left)
Katherine Kantor: pages 12 (elephant fish and skate), 14, 20 (bird skeleton)
Cori Marvin: page 12 (stingray)
Bonna Rouse: pages 6, 9 (right), 15 (all except mudpuppy), 21, 22, 31
Margaret Amy Salter: pages 18, 19
Doug Swinamer: page 20 (wings)
Tiffany Wybouw: pages 28, 29

Photographs
© Dreamstime.com: pages 17 (middle), 28, 30 (left)
© iStockphoto.com: pages 4 (backbone), 10 (top), 26 (skeleton), 27 (bottom), 31 (top left)
© 2008 Jupiterimages Corporation: page 31 (top right)
© ShutterStock.com: front cover, back cover, pages 3, 4 (fish and frog), 5 (lizard and boy), 7, 8 (top), 9, 10 (bottom), 11, 12, 13, 14, 15 (top), 16 (middle and bottom), 17 (top and bottom), 18, 19, 20, 21 (hummingbird and pelican), 22, 25, 26 (cats), 27 (top and middle), 29, 30 (right), 31 (middle right and bottom)
Other images by Corel, Digital Stock, Digital Vision, and Photodisc

Library and Archives Canada Cataloguing in Publication

Kalman, Bobbie, 1947-
    What is a vertebrate? / Bobbie Kalman.

(Big science ideas)
Includes index.
ISBN 978-0-7787-3277-8 (bound).
ISBN 978-0-7787-3297-6 (pbk.)

    1. Vertebrates--Juvenile literature. I. Title. II. Series.

QL605.3.K34 2007   j596   C2007-904739-4

Library of Congress Cataloging-in-Publication Data

Kalman, Bobbie.
    What is a vertebrate? / Bobbie Kalman.
      p. cm. -- (Big science ideas)
    Includes index.
    ISBN-13: 978-0-7787-3277-8 (rlb)
    ISBN-10: 0-7787-3277-0 (rlb)
    ISBN-13: 978-0-7787-3297-6 (pb)
    ISBN-10: 0-7787-3297-5 (pb)
    1. Vertebrates--Juvenile literature. I. Title. II. Series.

QL605.3.K35 2007
596--dc22

                                        2007030372

Crabtree Publishing Company
www.crabtreebooks.com   1-800-387-7650
Copyright © **2008 CRABTREE PUBLISHING COMPANY.** All rights reserved. No part of this publication may be reproduced, stored in a retrieval system or be transmitted in any form or by any means, electronic, mechanical, photocopying, recording, or otherwise, without the prior written permission of Crabtree Publishing Company. In Canada: We acknowledge the financial support of the Government of Canada through the Book Publishing Industry Development Program (BPIDP) for our publishing activities.

Published in Canada
Crabtree Publishing
616 Welland Ave.
St. Catharines, Ontario
L2M 5V6

Published in the United States
Crabtree Publishing
PMB16A
350 Fifth Ave., Suite 3308
New York, NY 10118

Published in the United Kingdom
Crabtree Publishing
Maritime House
Basin Road North, Hove
BN41 1WR

Published in Australia
Crabtree Publishing
386 Mt. Alexander Rd.
Ascot Vale (Melbourne)
VIC 3032

Contents

Bodies with bones

Animals have different bodies. Some animals have **backbones** inside their bodies. You have a backbone, too. Animals with backbones are called **vertebrates**. The animals shown here are all vertebrates.

a human backbone

A fish is a vertebrate.

*A frog is a vertebrate. Frogs belong to a group of animals called **amphibians**.*

There are five kinds of vertebrates. They are fish, amphibians, **reptiles**, birds, and **mammals**.

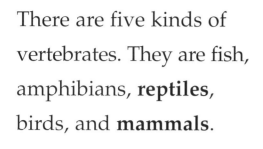

A parrot is a bird. Birds are vertebrates.

A lizard is a vertebrate. It is a reptile.

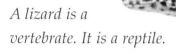

A dog is a vertebrate. People are vertebrates, too. Dogs and people are mammals.

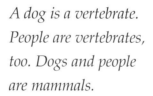

What is a skeleton?

Animals with backbones have many other bones inside their bodies, too. All the bones join together to make up a **skeleton**. A skeleton supports the body. The bones of the skeleton are covered with fat and skin. Your skeleton is made up of 206 bones! We also have **cartilage** in our bodies. Cartilage is like bone, but it bends. Your nose and ears are made of cartilage.

guinea pig

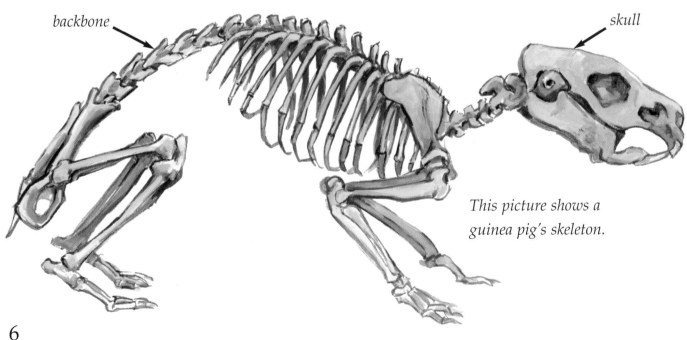

backbone

skull

This picture shows a guinea pig's skeleton.

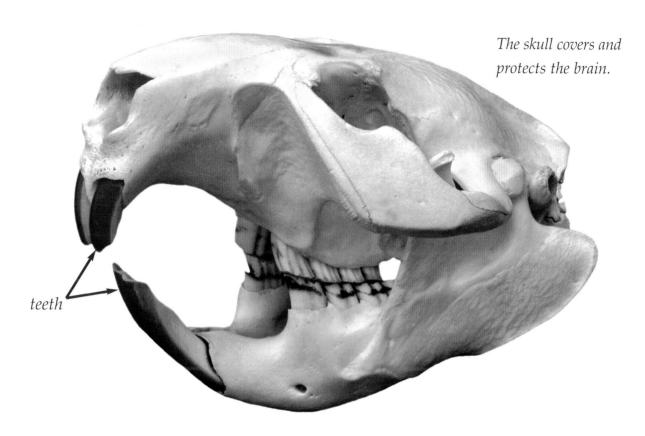

The skull covers and protects the brain.

teeth

Skulls inside

Most vertebrates have **skulls**. The skull is made up of bones that protect the head. The skull contains the mouth and teeth. Most vertebrates have teeth. The picture above shows a beaver's skull. Beavers have very long front teeth.

Beavers can cut down trees using their sharp front teeth.

7

More about bodies

Most vertebrates have eyes on their heads. Some vertebrates have eyes at the front of their heads. Some vertebrates have eyes at the side of their heads. The eyes of some birds are at the side of their heads. The eyes of a fox are at the front of its head.

Joints and muscles

Vertebrates have **joints** inside
their bodies. A joint is a place
where two bones come together.
Knees and elbows are joints. This koala
can climb because it has joints that bend.
Vertebrates also have **muscles**. Muscles give
vertebrates the strength to move their bodies.

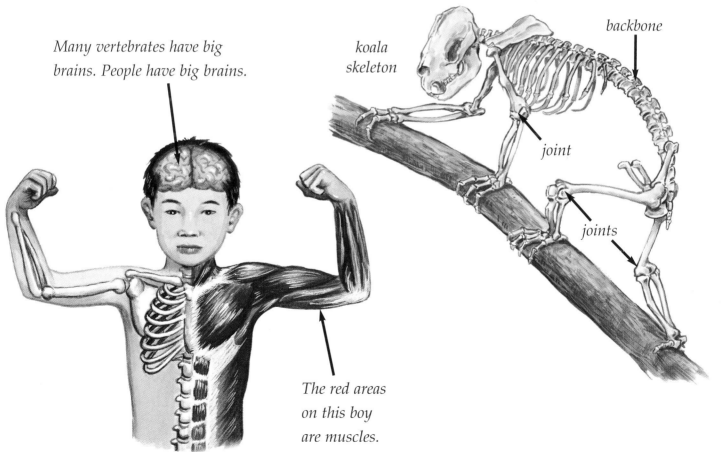

*Many vertebrates have big
brains. People have big brains.*

*koala
skeleton*

backbone

joint

joints

*The red areas
on this boy
are muscles.*

9

Fish backbones

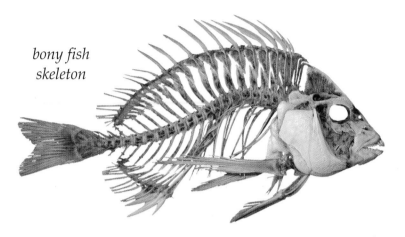

*bony fish
skeleton*

Fish are vertebrates that live in water. Most fish have skeletons made of hard bones. Fish with hard-bone skeletons are called **bony fish**.

10

fin

Fish swim

Fish have **fins** on their backs and sides. A fish's tail is a fin. Many fish move their tails from side to side when they swim. Their other fins help them turn and stop.

fin

This long fish is a trumpetfish.

The bodies of fish are made for swimming. Fish have muscles on the sides of their bodies. The fish above are moving their backbones and using their muscles to swim.

Skeletons that bend

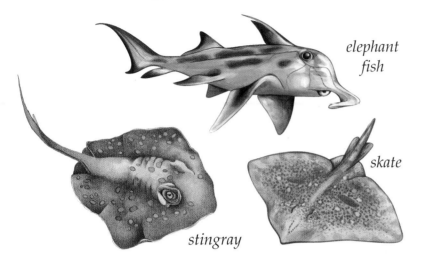

elephant fish

stingray

skate

Some fish do not have hard bones. Their skeletons are made totally of cartilage. Cartilage bends. Bone does not bend. The skeletons of rays, skates, and elephant fish are made of cartilage.

This eagle ray's skeleton is made of cartilage.

This fish's skeleton is made of hard bone.

Fast swimmers

The skeletons of sharks are made of cartilage, too. Cartilage is lighter than bone is. Cartilage helps sharks swim quickly. Sharks also have strong muscles to help them swim.

13

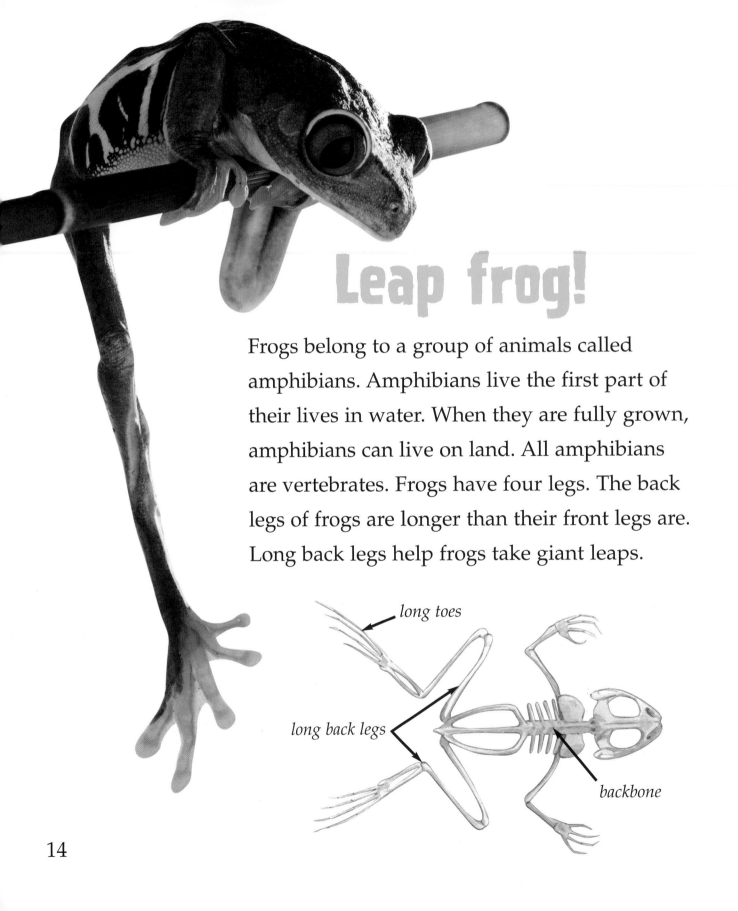

Leap frog!

Frogs belong to a group of animals called amphibians. Amphibians live the first part of their lives in water. When they are fully grown, amphibians can live on land. All amphibians are vertebrates. Frogs have four legs. The back legs of frogs are longer than their front legs are. Long back legs help frogs take giant leaps.

long toes

long back legs

backbone

Other amphibians

Toads, mudpuppies, salamanders, and newts are also amphibians. Unlike other amphibians, frogs and toads have no tails.

toad

mudpuppy

salamander

newt

Frogs use their legs to swim.

Frogs have long toes on their feet. Tree frogs use their legs and toes to climb trees.

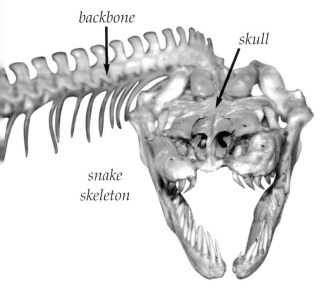

backbone

skull

snake
skeleton

Reptile bodies

Snakes belong to a group of animals called reptiles. Lizards are reptiles, too. All reptiles are vertebrates, but reptile bodies are not all the same. Snakes have no legs. They have long backbones with muscles around them. Snakes use their muscles to **slither** on the ground. To slither is to slide on the belly.

*All reptiles are covered with **scales**. A snake's scales are smooth.*

16

Big reptiles

Crocodiles and alligators are big reptiles. They have four legs with webbed feet for swimming. These big reptiles can live in water and also on land. They use their long, strong tails for swimming. Crocodiles and alligators use their powerful jaws to eat animals as big as deer. The jaw above is an alligator's jaw.

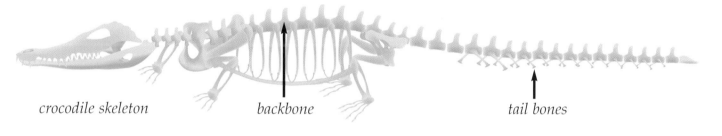

crocodile skeleton   *backbone*   *tail bones*

This young alligator will grow very large.

Reptiles with shells

Two kinds of reptiles have shells. Turtles and tortoises have shells. Both turtles and tortoises have backbones and skeletons inside their bodies. The shells cover their bodies. This tortoise and the turtle below both live on land.

tortoise

land turtle skeleton

shell

backbone

Box turtles and tortoises have legs. Their feet have claws.

box turtle

18

On land and in water

Tortoises and land turtles have legs, but sea turtles have **flippers** instead of legs. Flippers are for swimming. Sea turtles live in oceans and spend all their time swimming. Sea turtles could not swim as well if they had legs.

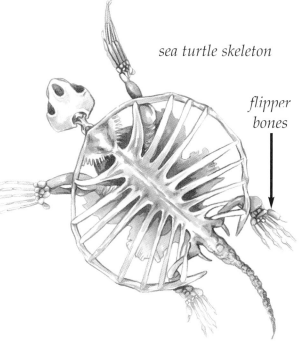

sea turtle skeleton

flipper bones

19

Birds have wings

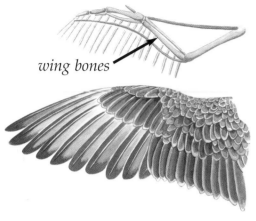

wing bones

backbone →

beak

joint

A bird has two legs, two wings, and a beak. Birds have no teeth. Most birds use their wings to fly. Birds have light bones. Their bones are light because they are hollow inside. Light bones do not weigh birds down while they fly.

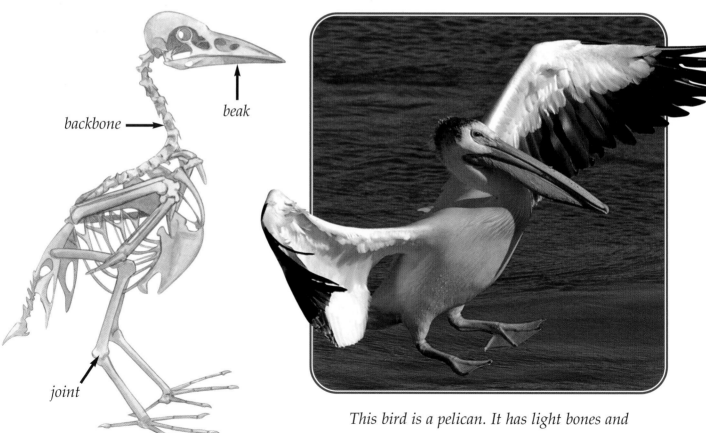

This bird is a pelican. It has light bones and big wings for flying. The bird is now landing.

Bird beaks

The beaks of birds are not all the same. The shape of a bird's beak helps a bird eat certain kinds of food. Egrets have long, thin beaks. They use their beaks like spears to catch animals such as fish, snakes, and crayfish. This egret has caught a frog to eat.

A hummingbird's long beak can reach nectar deep inside flowers.

A pelican can scoop up fish with its pouched beak.

An eagle's curved beak can tear meat.

Bird claws

Not all birds catch their food with their beaks. Birds called **raptors** catch their food with their claws. Raptors have big, strong claws.

21

Birds that do not fly

There are birds that do not fly. Their bodies and bones are made in a different way. Big birds cannot fly because their bodies are too large and heavy to stay in the air. Ostriches are too heavy to fly. Instead, they have strong legs for running fast. This ostrich has a big family! How many chicks are there?

Wings for swimming

These animals are not fish. They are birds called penguins. Penguins cannot fly. Penguins have wings like flippers. They use their wings to swim in oceans. Many penguins live in very cold places near oceans. They find fish to eat in ocean waters.

What are mammals?

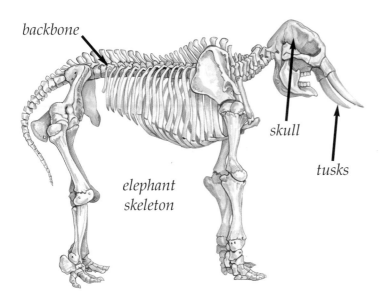

backbone

skull

tusks

*elephant
skeleton*

Mammals are vertebrates. Most mammals have fur or hair on their bodies. Mammals can be huge like this elephant. Mammals can be small like this mouse.

Walking on hoofs

Most mammals walk on four legs. Some mammals have **hoofs** on their feet. Animals with hoofs learn to stand and walk right after they are born. Horses have hoofs with one toe. Deer have two toes, and rhinos have three toes on their hoofs.

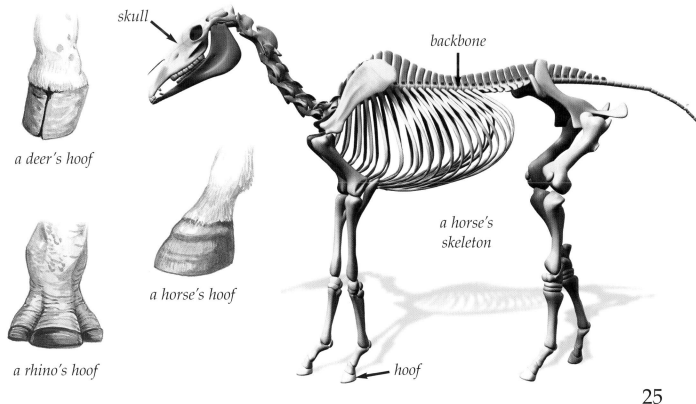

a deer's hoof

a rhino's hoof

a horse's hoof

skull

backbone

a horse's skeleton

hoof

Legs bend

Horses and elephants stand straight most of the time, but cats bend their legs a lot. A cat's joints and bones suit the way a cat moves.

Which of these cats has the same pose as this cat skeleton?

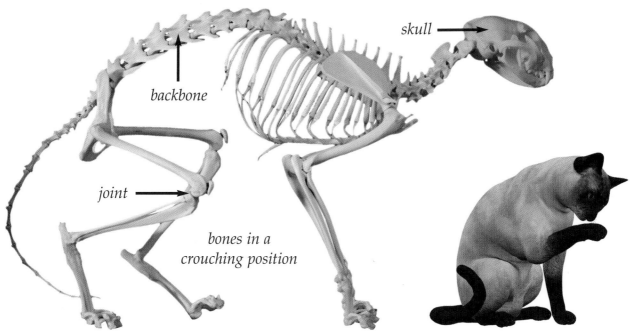

skull

backbone

joint

bones in a crouching position

26

Bunny hop

Some mammals walk, some run, and some hop. Bunnies hop. Their back legs are long, and they are bent. When the bunny straightens its back legs, it springs up and moves forward. Try hopping like a bunny. Bend your legs and then spring forward.

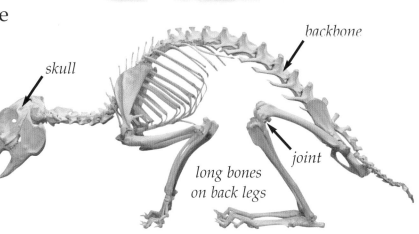

skull

backbone

joint

long bones on back legs

27

Mammals in oceans

Many mammals live on land, but some mammals live in oceans. Whales live in oceans. Dolphins are a kind of whale. Whales are mammals. Whales are vertebrates. Whales do not walk or hop. They have no legs. They have flippers instead of legs.

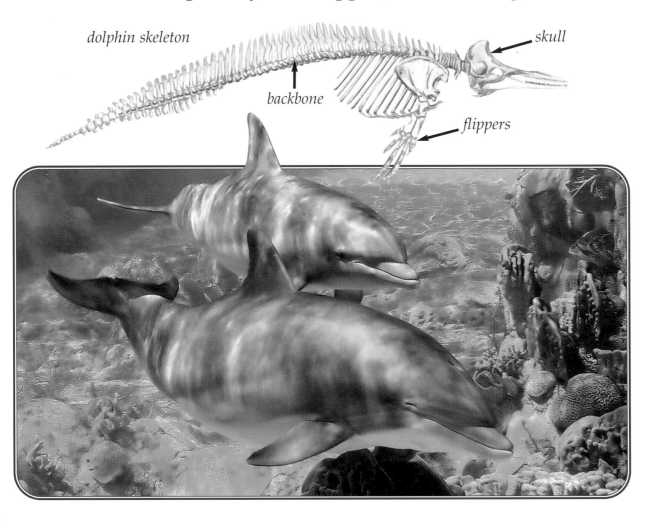

dolphin skeleton

skull

backbone

flippers

Dolphin moves

Fish move their tails from side to side, but dolphins and whales move their tails up and down. A dolphin's tail is like two legs and feet stuck together. Its flippers have finger bones inside. A long time ago, dolphins lived on land.

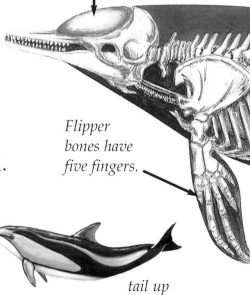

Dolphins have big brains.

Flipper bones have five fingers.

tail down

tail up

29

You are a vertebrate

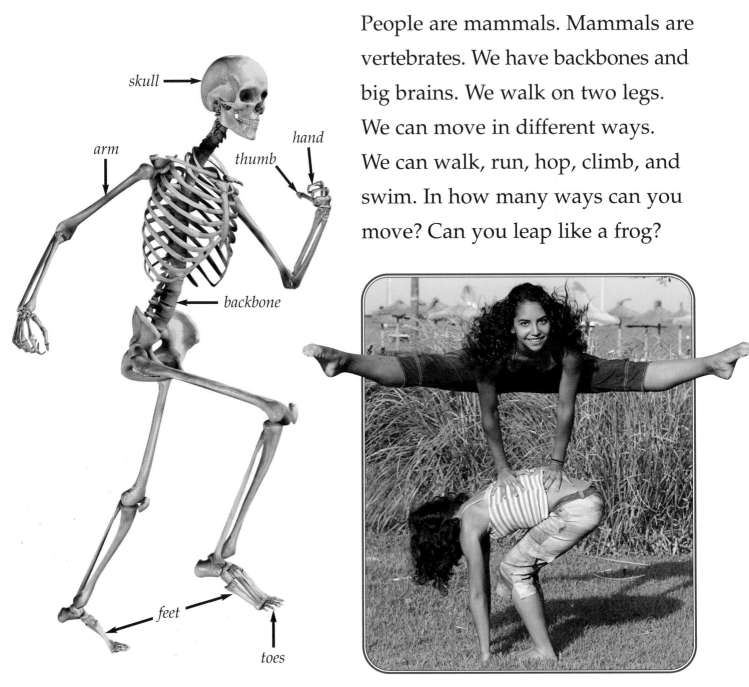

skull

arm

hand

thumb

backbone

feet

toes

People are mammals. Mammals are vertebrates. We have backbones and big brains. We walk on two legs. We can move in different ways. We can walk, run, hop, climb, and swim. In how many ways can you move? Can you leap like a frog?

Match these!

Which skeletons belong to which animals?

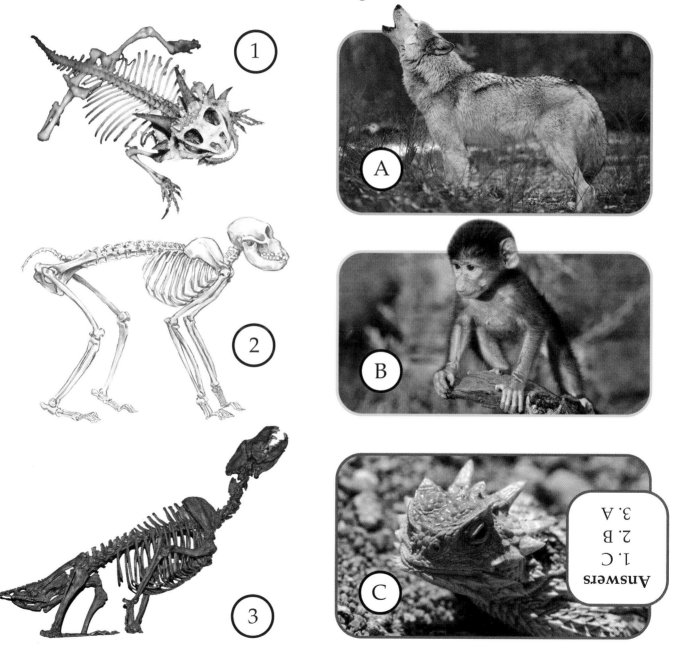

1

A

2

B

3

C

31

RICHMOND HEIGHTS

Glossary

Note: Some boldfaced words are defined in the book.

amphibian An animal such as a frog, which starts its life in water and can live on land as an adult

backbone The bones that run down from the head and which support the back

bony fish Fish that have skeletons made of hard bones that do not bend

cartilage Soft, bendable bonelike tissue that makes up the skeletons of some fish

flipper A broad, flat part on a sea animal such as a dolphin; used for swimming

mammal An animal with hair or fur, which has a backbone, breathes air, and drinks its mother's milk as a baby

muscle Part of the body that helps animals or people move and gives them strength

raptor A bird of prey, such as a hawk or owl, which uses its feet to catch prey

scales Small bony parts that protect the skin of fish and reptiles

skeleton A frame of bones inside an animal or person's body

skull Bones that cover a vertebrate's brain and contain the mouth and teeth

Index

Printed in the U.S.A.